Contents

Introduction	1
Chapter 1: Starting Out	4
Chapter 2: Planning and Prework	7
Chapter 3: Preliminary Mapping	16
Chapter 4: Mapping Event	39
Chapter 5: Identifying Opportunities	46
Chapter 6: Executing Initiatives	56
Chapter 7: Implementing Controls	59
Summary	62
Glossary	64
Step by Step Guide	69

Introduction

Once upon a time I was challenged to produce a Value Stream Map (VSM) in one day. Obviously, this was an impossible task to complete in that timeframe, so I negotiated an extra half day….

What I then had to do was come up with a way to create a map of the Value Stream that captured all the information that a full three-day session would and make sure nothing was left out. Over time I have been able to modify and improve my approach and I have included all the steps and details in this book. As time progressed, I found that I actually preferred this approach, as it gave me the opportunity to work more closely with Subject Matter Experts (SMEs), which in turn gave me better insights for the mapping exercise.

Most importantly, the techniques I outline here can be used by a first-time Mapper or a seasoned Lean Six Sigma Black Belt.

If you are unsure what the Value Stream is, it can be defined as a sequence of steps that happen to a product or service that adds value for the customer. If the customer wouldn't pay for a step, then why would we do it? This is an underpinning of the Lean Six Sigma philosophy and by eliminating steps that are unnecessary we remove waste, reduce variability and shorten cycle time. Creating a VSM gives us a picture of the steps that make up the Value Stream and allows us to pinpoint areas for improvement.

In 2016 there were 12 million workers, or around 8% of the total workforce in the U.S., engaged in Manufacturing (source: Bureau of Labor Statistics). The majority of books around improving processes seem to focus on this area, leaving a gap for the 92% of those engaged in other industries. The intent of this book is to focus on Transactional or "Back-office" processes rather than how a product is produced on the factory floor.

Too many times I have seen VSMs created for individual processes within the Value Stream without an overall high-level view of the Value Stream for the business. If you do not have that snapshot of the business, then I would recommend starting at that point. Think of this as an annual physical at the doctor's office. Mapping at this level will allow you to see the overall "health" of the business and will show areas the business needs to improve.

If you are already familiar with the Value Stream and know the areas in which you need to improve, then you can focus on those areas. Regardless of where you start, there are many benefits to be had from the high level VSM. Most importantly, it gives a clear, overall picture of what the business does, shows the structure of the Value Stream and can be used as a roadmap for future improvements. The high level VSM is extremely useful with executive groups to underline the need for continuous improvement, as it gives a concise graphic of how the business works and where the pain points are.

To summarize, the VSM process is as much an art as it is a science and there are many approaches that can be used. What I have covered here has worked effectively for me in the past and I am sure you will find them equally useful.

Chapter 1: Starting Out

A large number of Lean Six Sigma Black Belts and Green Belts work in an environment where a physical product is moved through the value stream with that product changing at each of those steps. Hopefully each of these steps add value to the product. This product is a *tangible* output that can be touched, picked up and physically examined at each step of the process. Transactional (Back-Office) processes, by their very nature, are *intangible*.

An invoice received electronically is *intangible* and cannot be touched, picked up or physically examined. The invoice exists as an electronic file and it is only when it is printed and you have a hardcopy that it would become *tangible*. The same is equally true of an electronic medical record or a sales forecast.

In today's world, we rely more and more on the electronic domain to let us do business or run our personal lives. Despite this, the mapping of a transactional process, although challenging, does not fundamentally differ from traditional Value Stream Mapping.

Contrary to popular belief, it doesn't take a Black Belt or Master Black Belt to create the VSM. The VSM is simply a tool that should be one of the first steps in the improvement process, as it gives a clear end-to-end view of the business process you want to examine. *Anyone* that can draw a box on a piece of paper can create a VSM. That said, this is not a project that can be completed by one person, as the map has to be created using the input from SMEs.

The person that facilitates the mapping (let's call them the Mapper) can only do so with the assistance and feedback from the SMEs, as they are the experts in the *process*. The Mapper should be the expert in the *tools* required to complete the VSM. You may not be there yet, but if you follow the guidelines here, and given enough practice, the tools will become second nature.

The easiest approach to Value Stream Mapping is to clearly define upfront the stages that are required. The six basic stages are **Planning and Prework, Preliminary Mapping, Mapping Event, Identifying Opportunities, Executing Initiatives** and **Implementing Controls**.

The first stage is **Planning and Prework** and the time spent here cannot be emphasized enough. Everyone has been involved in a project at some point in their career where the project stalled or was cancelled because clear goals and scope were not stated at the start of the project.

Preliminary Mapping is where my approach breaks from the traditional mapping process. This involves meeting one-on-one with each of the SMEs to create an initial map, based on their expert feedback.

The **Mapping Event** is a meeting of up to three days (although my approach condenses this to half that time) where the Value Stream Champion, SMEs and others involved in the process draw the Value Stream Map on Butcher paper (Craft paper can also be used) and will cover three maps; Current State, Ideal State and Future State.

From the maps we can begin **Identifying Opportunities** for improvement and create a prioritization of these initiatives so that the high impact projects are completed first.

Executing Initiatives covers how we approach the initiatives in a logical fashion to make sure that they are optimally implemented.

Implementing Controls covers how we put controls in place so that we maintain the improvements over time.

Chapter 2: Planning and Prework

As with any project, the prework is critical to success. Or to paraphrase the British SAS Special Forces Group, 'Proper Planning and Practice Prevent Pretty Poor Performance' (also known as the 7 P's).

Chances are you didn't decide to create a VSM because you were bored. All improvement initiatives start with a request to improve a process, eliminate a breakdown in the process or even completely redesign the process. This motivation could come from any number of reasons; days in accounts receivable are too high, customers complain about delivery time, quality is suffering and so on. The list is potentially endless… ..

For the Prework process you will want to create a Project Charter. The Charter will become the guiding document you will use to create structure around the VSM and for aligning resources. At a minimum, you need to identify the problem that you want to address, the Value Stream Champion, the scope of the mapping and also identify the SMEs and their managers.

Project Charter Outline

Problem Statement		
Value Stream Champion		
Mapping Leader	This is YOU...	
Scope		
Subject Matter Experts	SME Department	SME Manager

The first step in the Prework process, and arguably one of the most crucial parts, is to determine who in the organization decided the process needed assistance. This person could become the Value Stream Champion or they could assign someone else as Champion. The Champion is vital to your success, as it is up to them to create definition around the problem to be worked on, determine the scope of the mapping and who should be involved. They will also oversee how the changes will be executed, through Tollgate meetings.

Tollgate (or Project Review) meetings take place after the team has identified specific projects to improve the process.

The goals of the meeting are to determine how effective the ongoing changes have been and whether they are on-track.

The Champion serves the role of clearing obstacles from your path and allows you to concentrate on the task at hand - creating the VSM. In general, the Champion tends to be someone at an upper management level that has the influence within the business to make changes and ensure they are implemented. Champions are typically at the Vice President or Director level. You can see that already we are putting structure around what we want to accomplish.

During the Planning and Prework phase you will meet with the Champion several times and through this interaction you will become the "Trusted Advisor" to the Champion. At this stage in the process, the Champion will be guiding you to the various pieces of information and data you will need to gather, but this is very much a partnership between you and the Champion to determine what is needed for the mapping. The Champion will be able to walk you through the main process areas that will need to be included, as well as giving you guidance as to the Problem Statement and the Key Performance Indicators (KPIs).

For an initial high-level mapping of the business, you would want to focus on the External Customer. As you become more familiar and skilled at mapping, you will be tackling specific processes *within* the business. This means your customer will change, depending on what part of the Value Stream you are mapping. The Internal Customer will be the department (or person) that is downstream of the final step in the process. A good example would be Human Resources data for new hires. Mostly, I.T. uses that data for the on-boarding process which would make them your Customer.

You will want the Problem Statement to be very specific in the details. What is the issue, where does it happen, who affects the process, how does the process affect the customer and how does the process affect the business? For our example, the problem statement could be "Customers receive invoices late, creating problems for them to process invoices in a timely fashion resulting in an increase in the number of days in Accounts Receivable". So, we have captured the impacts in the problem statement that affect the Customer *and* the Business.

Having identified the Value Stream Champion and collaborated with them to create the problem statement, the next step is to set the project scope and determine which areas of the business need to be included in the VSM. From here, the Champion will help to identify the individuals that will represent these areas. Discussing the process with the Champion will help identify the major process steps involved in the Value Stream. The main areas in our example of invoice processing could be

Sales & Marketing, the Quote process, Finance, Accounting and Information Technology (I.T.).

One pitfall a lot of people fall into is selecting only senior managers for the team. Senior management will understand the broad strokes of the process but may be unaware of how the process truly happens because it has changed dramatically since they were last involved directly. To be able to get access to the level of detail you require for the VSM, you need that frontline knowledge of how the process works on an hour-by-hour, week-by-week, month-by-month basis that you can only get from those that DO the work; they are the true SMEs of the process. This is not to say you would exclude managers of the SMEs from the team, but you want to be careful that you do not end up with a group so large that it becomes difficult to manage. It is also possible the SMEs that are chosen will not be comfortable about critiquing the process in front of their manager. Remember that the purpose of the VSM is to document current state, so honest and frank feedback as to how the current state works is critical. Part of your role as Mapper will be to coax that information from the SMEs using questions that probe their knowledge of the process.

It is important to differentiate the process from the person. People, with the best of intentions, will continue to use a broken process because they either cannot affect change or do not know how. This in no way means that those involved are not hard-working, conscientious people and given the opportunity, they would prefer to be able to work effectively.

Project scope sets the start and end points for the mapping process, as well as giving boundaries for the mapping. With the best of intentions, you will find SMEs or managers that may want to include or exclude other areas of the business, introducing "Scope Creep" into the process. "Scope Creep" is when the original scope of the mapping begins to change. Typically, this change would be including areas that were not in the original scope and could involve expanding either the start or end points of the process. Clear definition of the scope helps to keep the team on track. When you talk to them, having predetermined start and end points for the mapping allows you to address any additional areas they may want to include as being other potential projects or mapping exercises, but are not covered under the current scope. In other words, 'we hear you, but we have to stick to the scope, otherwise we'll get off-track and lose momentum. The points you raise are valid and we will investigate these issues further when we have completed the mapping'. Many times, additional mappings and projects will come from these nuggets of information.

The next step of the Prework will be contacting the SME's managers for their approval to release them for the mapping. The mapping process will be one and a half days, so this approval is important. Not only is this a common courtesy, but it communicates the time commitment to the managers and underlines the importance of the mapping exercise. Occasionally you will encounter a manager who can't release an SME to participate in the mapping. If the reasons are fair and legitimate, the manager should be able to give you a substitute SME. If not, then you will have to get the Champion involved to make sure you have SME coverage from that area of the business.

With the Champion and SMEs identified, you can now begin to fill in the charter document with the problem statement that drives the reason for the mapping, the project scope and the SMEs that were chosen for the team Page 8 includes a framework for the Charter and it can be created in MS Word or MS Excel, whichever you are most comfortable with. The Project Charter will be a dynamic, living document up until the day of the Mapping Event. From experience, last minute conflicts may change the list of SMEs, other SMEs may be added and other managers added. It's important to be flexible and remember that this preparation is setting you up for success.

Since you have already identified the Champion, this person should be added to the charter. From your initial conversations with the Champion, the Problem Statement and scope of the project have already been fleshed out. Add these to the charter. Add each selected team member and their department to the charter, along with the person they report to. The example below is a completed high-level charter. For your purposes, you could expand as necessary to cover the benefits to the business, benefits to the customer, individual metrics and so on. However, for our example, the details captured are sufficient. There are multiple versions of Project Charters in use and your organization may well have a template that you prefer to use.

Project Charter Example

Problem Statement	Customers receive invoices late, creating problems for them processing invoices in a timely fashion resulting in an increase in the number of days in Accounts Receivable	
Value Stream Champion	Fred Smith, VP Finance	
Mapping Leader	This is YOU…	
Scope	**Start:** Sales Team signs up a new customer	**End:** I.T. transmits electronic invoice to the customer
Subject Matter Experts	**SME Department**	**SME Manager**
Mary Smith	Customer Service	Harry Brown
Fred Jones	Quotations	John Green
Ken Murphy	Finance	Fred Smith
Mike O'Brien	I.T.	Curtis Jones
Dave Smith	Sales & Marketing	Joan Ortiz

Once the SMEs have been selected and you have approval for their participation, you will want to have a brief one-on-one conversation with them to introduce yourself, give them an overview of what a VSM is and what the mapping will and will not cover (the project scope). The completed Project Charter can be used to review with each of the SMEs. They have been selected for their expert knowledge of the process and the mapping will allow them to share this knowledge with the group and improve the process at hand. Now you can now begin focusing on the Preliminary Mapping......

Chapter 3: Preliminary Mapping

In the traditional form, a ten to fifteen-foot length of Butcher paper is taped to one wall of the room being used and the various components of the map are drawn on the blank paper as the map progresses. Supplier boxes, customer boxes, process boxes and all the data and process steps are all gradually added to the map. Current state of the process is mapped, followed by Ideal and Future states. Laid out this way, the mapping event will take the full three days. Obviously, this takes a considerable time commitment from the Champion, team members and managers.

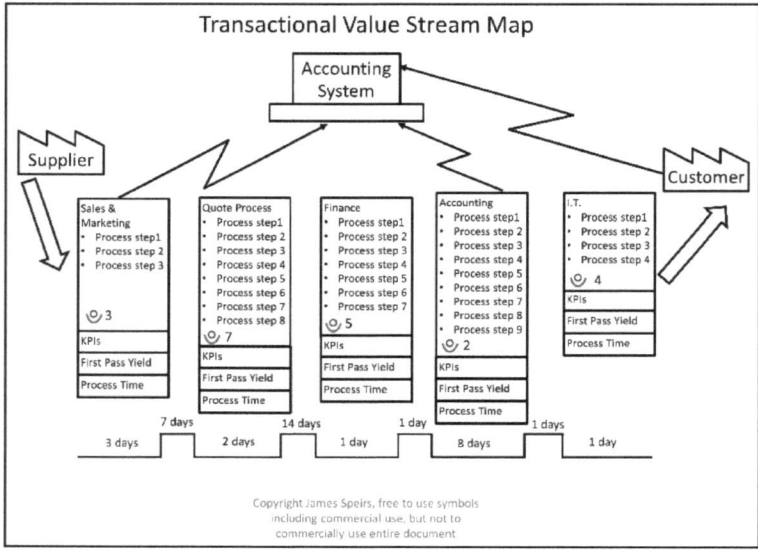

This is all fine and well and adheres to the mapping process that Toyota (and others) originally used when they pioneered the use of the VSM. However, in the real world it is not often possible to get that time commitment from all involved.

During the Mapping Event the Champion may have to leave the room. As they are the executive sponsor of the Mapping Event, they could have other pressing business issues to deal with. However, the SMEs and managers need to be there for the entire event so that they hear all the feedback from the team, to ensure maximum participation.

From experience, a lot of the time spent mapping is taken up with valuable dialogue between team members that allows us to fine-tune the map to a true representation of Current state. When I began to work directly with external customers it became apparent that we couldn't realistically expect the customer to carve out three days from their schedules. To meet this challenge, I developed a faster method of creating the VSM, but still gathering all the much-needed information and feedback. It occurred to me to start with a VSM that was *already* completed, essentially *Leaning* a Lean process. This approach decreases the mapping time since we start the Mapping Event with an already completed map, reducing the amount of time that the team needs to spend in the Mapping Event. The benefits of this to the customer are obvious and when you are working with internal resources, this approach minimizes the impact of them being away from their day-to-day jobs.

As I said earlier, the ability to create a valid Current State map is down to having SME and manager feedback, without which, the map is basically a "best-guess". I simply moved the work around to where I would interview SMEs, create a preliminary map and reduce the time needed for the Mapping Event.

Information needed to build the VSM falls into four basic categories; Supplier and Customer boxes, Process and Metrics boxes, Information flows and Lead and Queue times.

My accelerated approach starts by interviewing in turn each SME to begin the Preliminary Map. Usually, you can get the information from the SME in a one-hour meeting, or less. You want to ask them about the steps they perform in order to complete their part of the process. Again, relatively high level, as this is not a detailed process map. Next, you want them to tell you how many people work on the process and about the information flows of their part of the process; completing Excel spreadsheets, updating computer systems and any other paperwork they touch are all things you should gather. You may have captured these activities in the Process Box, but you also want to see how the information *flows* across the Value Stream. Finally, you want to capture the Key Performance Indicators

(KPIs), First Pass Yield, Process times, Lead times and Queue times for their process. KPIs can be a delicate subject, as the SME will have a good idea of where the breakdowns are and may be cautious about sharing this information. This is where it is important for you to explain that the map is about the *process*, not the *person*.

During the interview with the SME, I have always found it beneficial to draw their process box on a whiteboard or flip chart. This gives the SME a better understanding of what you are trying to create and is less intimidating if they have that visual. With all this information gathered, the data can be transferred to a separate document or you can begin drawing the preliminary map. Microsoft Visio is a convenient tool to create the map in, but it can be also created in MS PowerPoint, which most people have access to.

Once the first process box is completed from the information the SME has given you, move onto the next SME interview and repeat the process until all SMEs are interviewed and process boxes, information flows and KPIs are populated. Now you can begin to create a rough VSM, based on the SME feedback (see pages 20 – 22). When you create your VSM you will want to start with framing the map with the Supplier on the far left and the Customer on the far right. With that done you can then draw the Process boxes and other elements of the VSM.

Step 1:

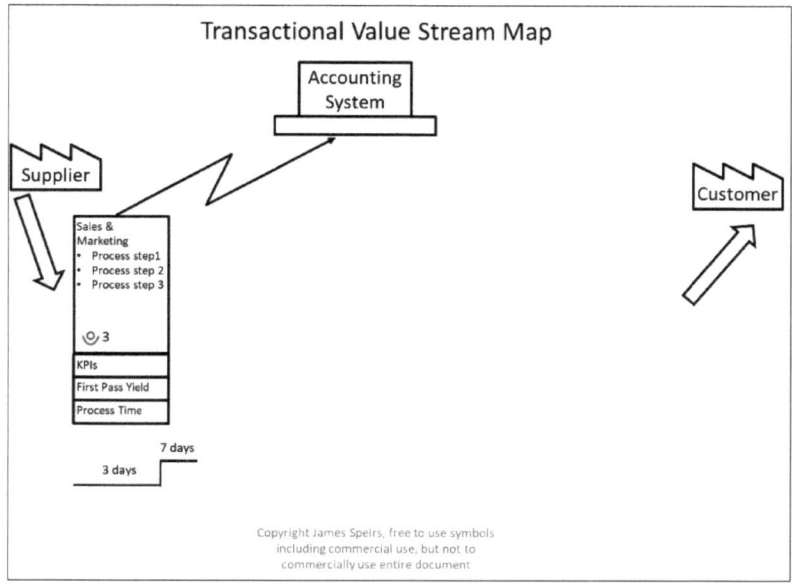

Step 2:

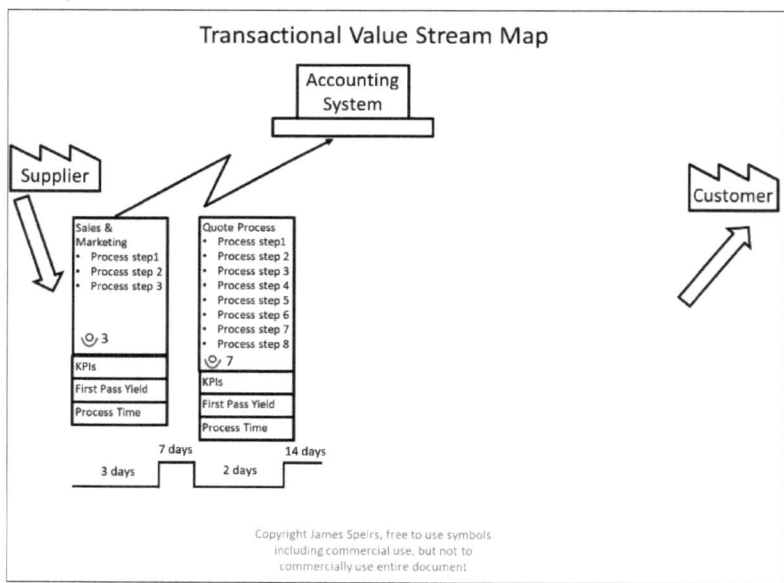

Step 3:

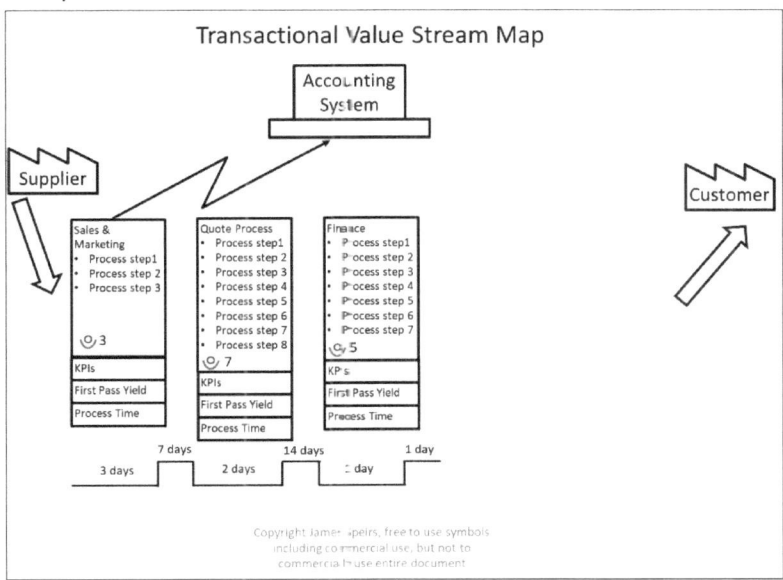

Step 4:

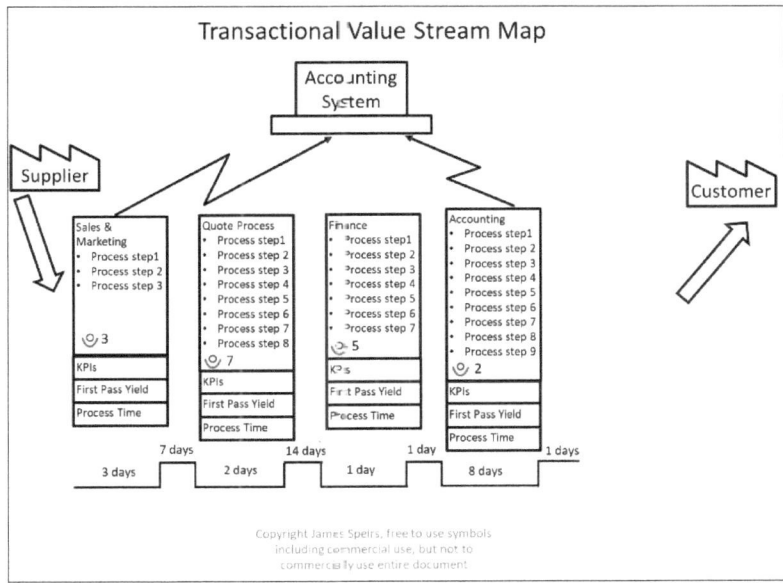

Step 5:

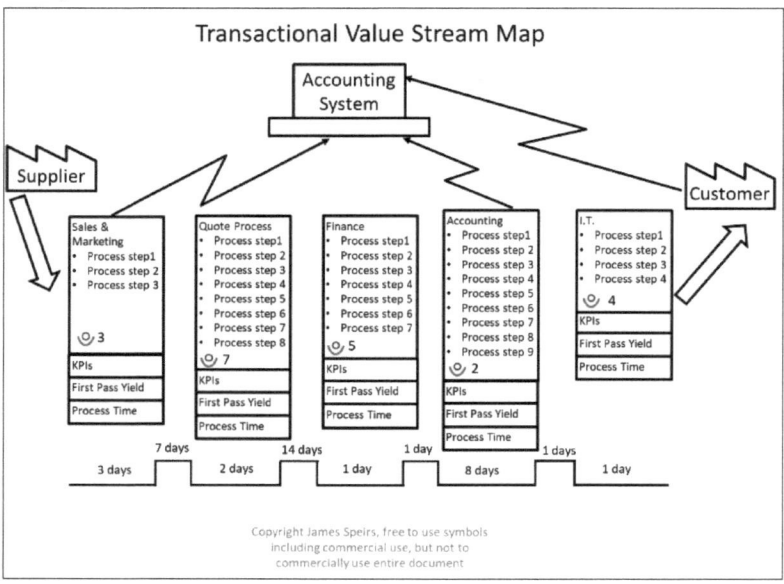

Supplier and Customer Boxes

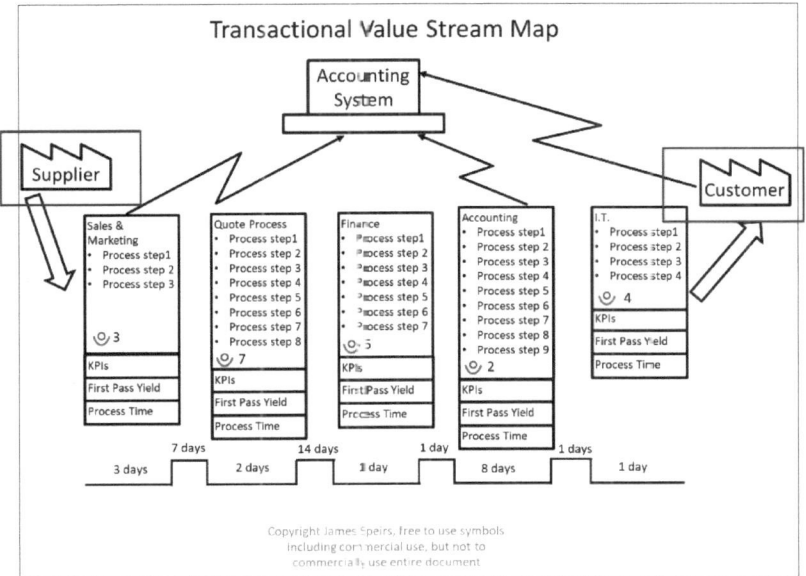

Supplier and Customer boxes sit on the left and righthand sides of the VSM, respectively, and show the Supplier to the Value Stream and the end Customer of the Value Stream. For our invoice example, the Supplier would be the area of the business that provided the service that was utilized by the customer. The Customer would be the end Customer for that service.

Process Boxes

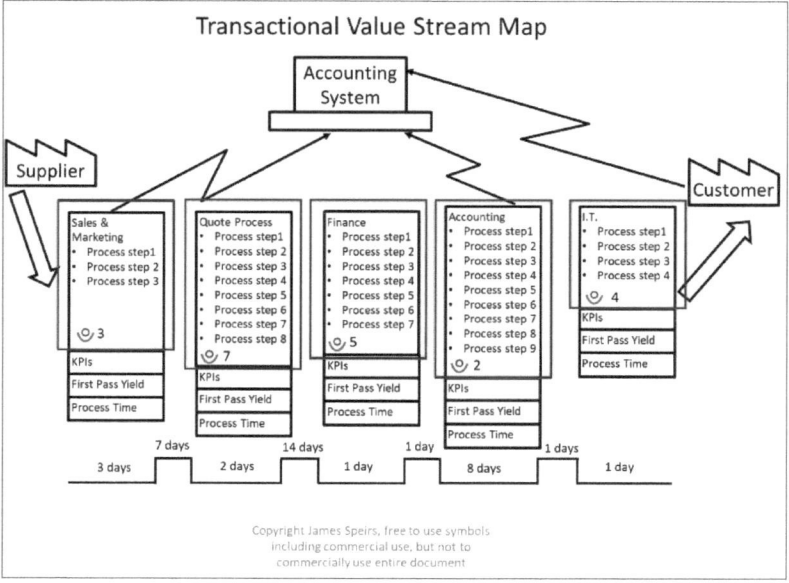

Each Process Box captures the time-ordered, chronological process steps and represents work that is done to move the output to the next step. For a first time Mapper this can be daunting, as you want a certain amount of detail, but not every detail. If someone is putting information into a database, you don't want to capture every keystroke and every time they hit "Enter".

Imagine a Mail Room processing daily mail. Typical steps could be:

- Put mail bins at the Sorting Station
- Sort mail into departments
- Place sorted mail in department bins
- Place bins on mail cart
- Deliver mail

Any process steps more detailed than this would be better captured in a process map, not a VSM.

The number of steps in the box is not governed by any hard and fast rule; you could have three steps or you could have twelve or more. This is where the SME feedback from the interviews will guide you. The level of detail is such that you don't want to record every keystroke for entering data into a database, but rather the fact that a database was used. You also want to get from the SME the total number of people involved in their process step. The semi-circle with the "O" in the center is the "People" icon and denotes the number of people involved with that process. If you have seven Quote Specialists, then put a "7" beside the People icon, if you have three sales people, put a "3" beside the People icon.

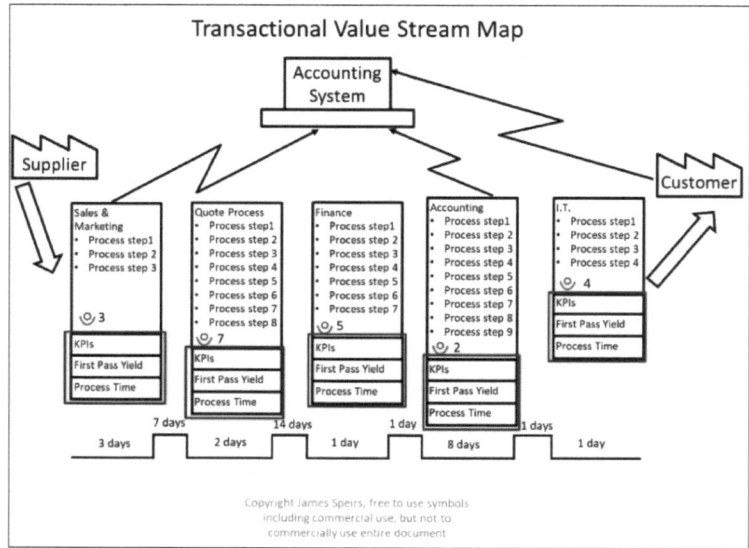

At the bottom of each of the Process boxes are the metrics that describe how that Process box performs and there are three basic pieces of data for a transactional VSM:

- Key Performance Indicators (KPIs) – This can be one or more measurable values of how the process performs. Rather than create a new metric, it is easier to use the existing metric for how the process is already being measured. Enter in the KPI line the KPI the SME for that process gave you during the time you interviewed them. It could be "Number of Invoices processed daily" or "% Corrected invoices". Remember, the KPI for that Process Box is the metric that the SME is held accountable to, or the measurement of success for that process.

The next line is "First Pass Yield" or the percent of the process that happens the first time with no rework, hinderance or other intervention. In other words, a perfect scenario.

- First Pass Yield (FPY) – This is defined as the percentage of time that the process runs through, from start to finish, unhindered. If the SME processed 100 invoices per day, how many can be passed to the next step of the process with no reworking? If the answer is 78 invoices, then this would be 78% (78 invoices divided by 100 invoices)

FPY and its big brother, Rolled Throughput Yield (RTY) are measurements that aren't often used in a transactional VSM, but I have found them extremely useful in helping the team get a better understanding about their processes. We'll cover both these in greater depth, further on.

Process Time goes on the final line and is the time it takes if the process could be started and followed to completion with no delays or interruptions. As a guideline, I always ask the SME 'if you could start working on the process at 8:00 a.m. on Monday morning and you were able to work through the process with no interruptions, when would you finish?'.

o   Process Time – The amount of time it takes for the process to execute *in a perfect world*.

Information Flows

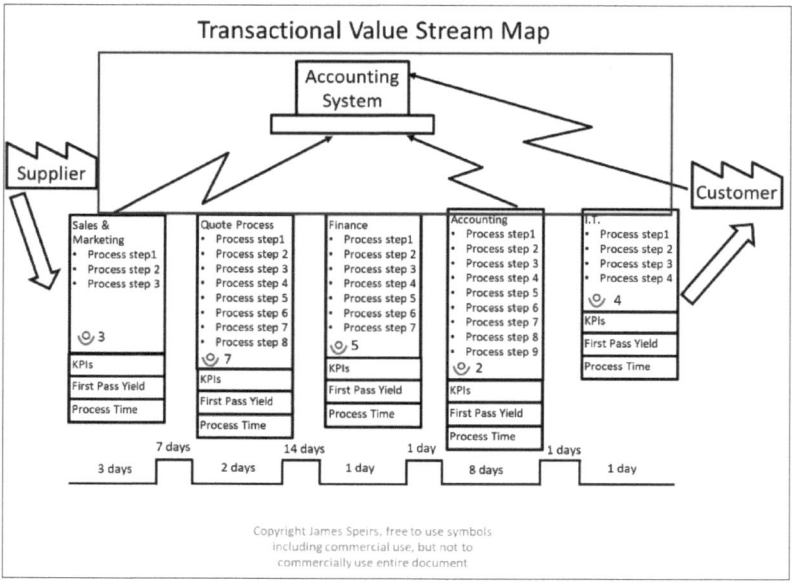

Now you can move to the Information Flows at the top of the map. The intent here is to capture how all the information flows from the Process Boxes to the various systems that are used. Any time someone uses a computer during the process, they are making information flow through the system for that process. It could be accessing a database on a server or mainframe computer or sending a Fax or using Excel to create a sales forecast. You will want to capture all these electronic systems here.

- Information flows track the movement of information across the Value Stream. This could be either electronic information, such as data entry into a computer system or the manual movement of information, such as a hardcopy invoice being mailed.

System boxes are joined to the Process boxes using the Lightning Bolt arrows that show the direction of the information flow. This shows that that an electronic process is being used. Information flow doesn't always have to be electronic and could involve mailing a hardcopy invoice to a customer. Capture any of these types of non-electronic flows, but this time, use a straight arrow to show they are non-electronic flows of information.

Lead Times and Queue Times

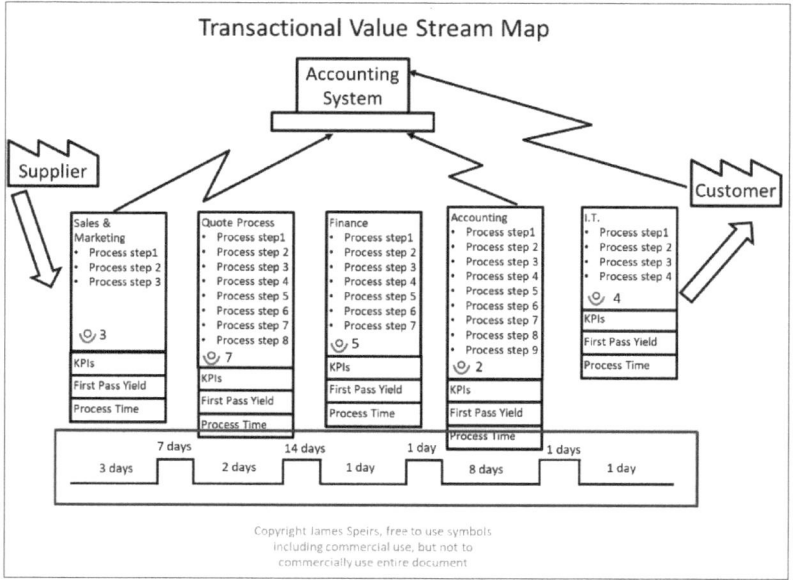

The final stage will be completing the Lead times and Queue times. Lead time sits on the lower stepped line directly under the Process Box and Queue time is put on the upper stepped line between Process Boxes.

- o Lead time represents the actual amount of time the process takes to execute from start to finish. The time it takes Finance to process an invoice could be twenty minutes, but the Lead time could be eight hours because of other work they have to complete during the day. This differs from the Process time, in that this is "actual" versus "perfection".

- Queue time is the amount of wait time from the end of the previous process until the next process begins. It can be elusive to fully quantify as the person completing the process may not know when the next step begins. However, the person downstream will know when they start their process, so taking information from both SMEs will allow you to more closely determine an accurate Queue time

Not all processes will have a measurable Queue time, especially in the Transactional world. If the product you are moving through the Value Stream is electronic in nature (files, requests, etc.) then they could be instantly available to the next part of the process. However, you may find that even though a file is available on a server or e-mailed by 3:00 p.m. each day, the next person in the process may not begin to work on them until noon on the next day.

The graphics on pages 20 to 22 show how the map progresses as the input from each SME is added, finally ending up with a completed map.

To make sure all the information around each process is captured, you will want to meet briefly with each SME one last time, to review the Preliminary Map before the mapping session.

Essentially you have now reduced the entire first day of the Mapping session to a Vetting session of the map, which should probably take two hours. Instead of starting to map the process on a blank piece of paper during the Mapping Event, you already have the preliminary map created and have made significant progress.

To make sure what you have captured is a fair and accurate representation of the process, it's always advisable to see the process working. The best time to do this is after your initial meeting with the SME. From the first meeting, you will have already met the SME and any observation of the process will be far less intrusive.

The "Gemba Walk" is a Lean technique that means "the real place" in Japanese. This involves going to where the work is done (and value is added to the process) and actually observing the process in real time. The "Gemba Walk" allows the Mapper to see the process firsthand and this serves as a reality check for what you will be mapping. Originally developed for observing shop-floor processes, it is an equally effective tool for the transactional environment and is something you will want to do at some point prior to the Mapping Event. Despite the best efforts of the SMEs to describe their process and hand-offs, occasionally they can be too close to the process and may miss some crucial steps.

In our invoice example, you would want to sit beside the person doing the work for each of the process steps and observe what work is being done. You want to be as unobtrusive as possible as you want to only observe and not make suggestions as to how the process could be approached more effectively. Although the Mapper should absolutely not be making changes to the preliminary map without working directly with the SMEs, this opportunity gives you a better insight as to appropriate probing questions to ask during the mapping session.

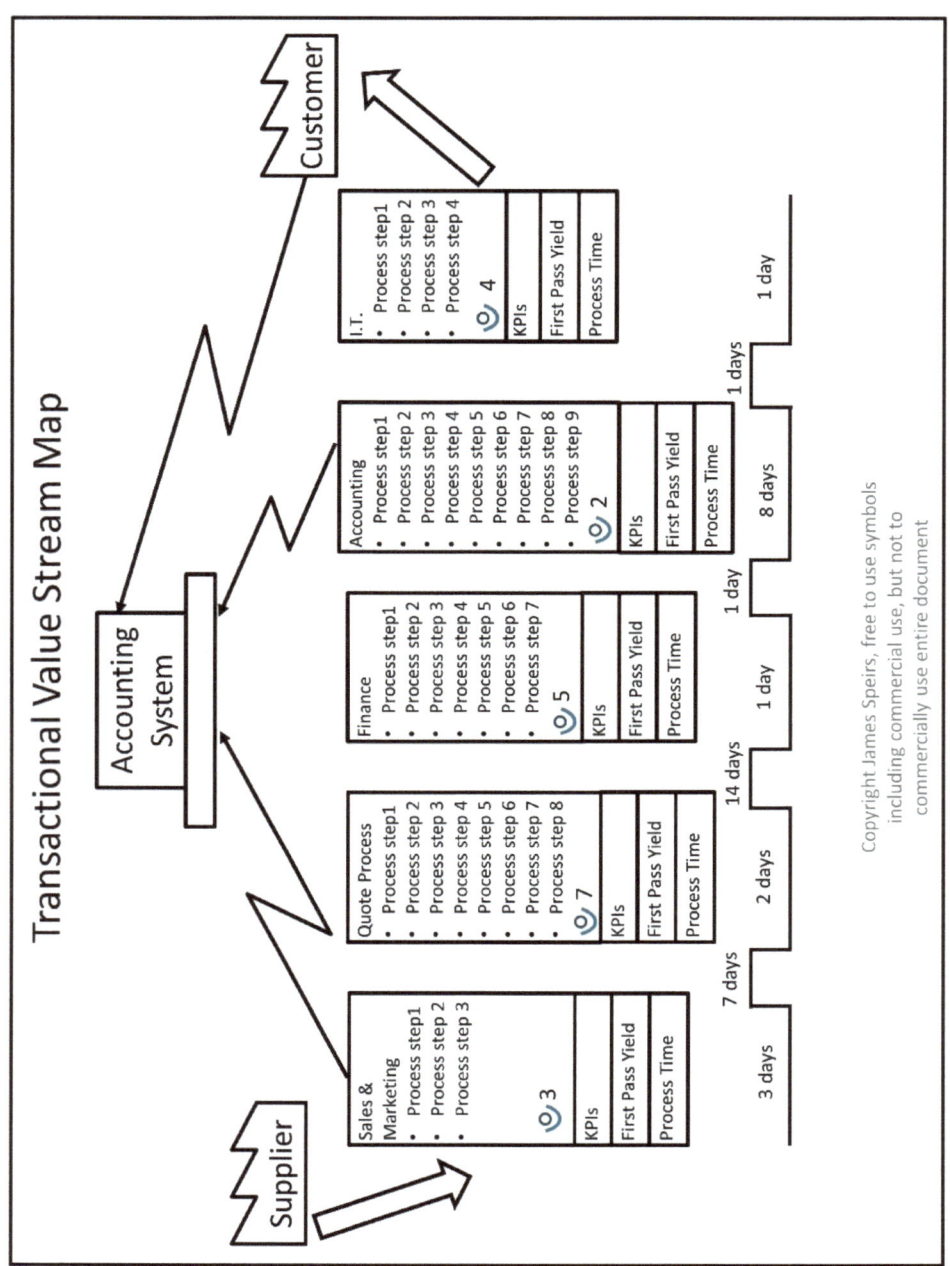

When you have finished with all the SME interviews and have their feedback that what you have captured is a fair representation of what they shared with you, you will want to print a 48" x 36" copy for the Mapping Event. If you don't have access to a large format printer, Kinkos and Office Depot can print large sizes from an electronic file. That said, there is absolutely no issue with hand-drawing the map on a sufficiently large piece of paper.

The VSM template on the previous page shows how we took our invoice problem from the earlier example and created a VSM from SME feedback.

It can take up to two weeks to complete the preliminary mapping. Remember that you will need to meet twice with each SME and the number of SMEs you need to interview will depend upon the number of Process Boxes you need to complete. One thing to bear in mind is the availability of the SMEs and the fact that this may not be their most pressing issue.

Congratulations! Your preliminary Value Stream Map is complete and ready for the next step.

Prior to the Mapping Event, you will want to create an agenda for the Mapping Event. By doing this, it will give you a structure with which you can plan the event. The agenda can be sent several days prior to the event to all the team members.

Agenda examples are shown on pages 37 and 38, and as always, nothing is written in stone, so you can modify these examples to meet the needs of your event.

Day One

Attendees: Fred Jones, Ken Murphy, Mike O'Brien, Dave Smith, Fred Smith, Mary Smith, Mapper

Time		
8:00 a.m. – 8:15 a.m.	Introductions, Expectations and Overview	Mapper
8:15 a.m. – 10:15 a.m.	Review Current State Map	Mapper / All
10:15 a.m. – 10:30 a.m.	Break	All
10:30 a.m. – 12:30 p.m.	Create Ideal State Map	All
12:30 p.m. – 1:00 p.m.	Lunch	All
1:00 p.m. – 3:00 p.m.	Create Future State Map	All
3:00 p.m. – 3:15 p.m.	Break	All
3:15 p.m. – 4:00 p.m.	Identify Opportunities	All
4:00 p.m. – 4:30 p.m.	Summarize the Day	All

Day Two

Attendees: Fred Jones, Ken Murphy, Mike O'Brien, Dave Smith, Fred Smith Mary Smith, Mapper

Time		
8:00 a.m.– 8:15 a.m.	**Review the Previous Day**	Mapper
8:15 a.m. – 10:15 a.m.	**Prioritize Opportunities**	Mapper / All
10:15 a.m. – 10:30 a.m.	**Break**	All
10:30 a.m. – 11:30 a.m.	**Assign Opportunities**	All
11:30 a.m. – 12:00 p.m.	**Next Steps & Wrap Up**	All

Chapter 4: Mapping Event

On the first day of the VSM, you will want to put the preliminary map on the wall so the entire group can see the end to end Value Stream. You also want to create a "Parking Lot" list on a flipchart or whiteboard. The purpose of the "Parking Lot" is to capture points that are raised by the team that you may not want to pursue at the time they are raised. You definitely want to make sure all these thoughts and points brought up are documented so they are not lost.

Begin the session with introductions and have everyone in the room introduce themselves and give a brief overview of their role in the Value Stream. Depending upon how well the group knows each other, you could throw in a quick five-minute "Ice-Breaker"; 'If you won $500M in the Lottery, what would you buy first' or 'What's your favorite hobby?'. Anything that gets the group interaction moving along is always helpful.

Having completed the introductions and "Ice-Breaker" exercise, you can then begin to walk through the map, starting with the Supplier and end Customer, moving on to the individual Process boxes and each step captured in the Process boxes. Walk the team through each of the individual process steps in the Process Boxes and each of the KPIs, FPY and Process times (it's always easier to work from left to right across the

Value Stream). Since the information flows have a broader impact across the Value Stream, it's easier to review them last.

At each step of the Vetting, you will want to ask the group to comment on whether the VSM has captured a fair representation of the process. Reaching consensus around this is crucial, since not everyone will agree with how the map shows the process. If you reach a point where the team in general agree, but one or two team members do not, then the question is; can they accept what has been mapped, even though they may not fully agree? This is an important step, as it can be really easy to become bogged down on minutia and bring discussion to a halt. One way around this is to call a short break and resume the discussion when the team returns. If there is still an impasse, you will want to note these points on the Parking Lot and move onto the next part of the map. At this stage in the mapping it's important to maintain momentum rather than drag the team into a lengthy discussion, when you can revisit these points later.

As you walk through the VSM with the team, any changes can be easily made directly on the map with a marker, as you want to create as accurate a picture of Current State as is possible. Once the Vetting is complete, you will want to take pictures (lots of them!) of the completed Current State map, as creating the Future State map will involve making changes directly on the Current State map.

Now for a bit of controversy. The Mapping Event should cover the creation (or Vetting, in this case) of the Current State VSM. From there you can move on to creating an Ideal State map and then return to the Current State map to create Future State. The Ideal State map challenges the team to create a map for the Value Stream that exists in an ideal Utopian state. In this situation you would have unlimited resources, unlimited funding and basically, the sky is the limit. This exercise is intended to create something that, from a process standpoint, is always on the horizon, just out of grasp. In my experience, I have found this can be a welcome break in the middle of dealing with the constraints of reality and it gets the team thinking in broader terms of how they could more creatively approach problems.

Teams can have a negative reaction to this and may view it as essentially a waste of time in what is a full agenda. Even discussing this with Lean Six Sigma experts, there are a lot of mixed views on whether or not to map Ideal State. Since you have already met and interviewed all the SMEs in the mapping, you should have a good idea as to whether this is a team that would benefit from mapping the Ideal State or would find it pointless. One real world example I encountered was when I created an Ideal State map with a team, where they decided to use Uber drivers rather than company trucks. What this did was get the team thinking about existing transportation problems in the Current State that they then quickly addressed when we mapped Future State. Without this coming up in the Ideal State, it's entirely possible that we would not have had the same emphasis on the transportation side. I shall leave the choice up to you for mapping Ideal State.....

If you have decided to create an Ideal State map with the team, you would do so at this point. The time to complete the Ideal State map can vary, but I have always found that it's best to allocate about two hours to this. Most times you will finish sooner than that, but it is always best to set aside more time, rather than rush through other agenda topics.

Tape a piece of Butcher paper, about 60" to 72" long, to the wall. Draw the Supplier box on the far left and the Customer box on the far right. Now you can begin with the first Process Box. Refer to the Current State map and ask the team if the first Process Box from Current State would even exist in an Ideal State. If it does, then draw the box and ask the team for the processes that would happen in that box, under an Ideal State. Continue to complete the processes and then address the KPIs, FPY and Process Time. In an Ideal state, what would these be? Once complete, move on to the next Process Box. During this exercise, you are simply drawing what the team directs you to draw and asking questions around why would it be there and what purpose does it serve? Continue with the Process Boxes and then populate the Lead and Queue times along the bottom.

Then you can conclude with the Information Flows at the top. And remember, anything is possible; this is Ideal State.

Whether or not you decided to map the Ideal State, you would now begin to create the Future State map. This part of the mapping revolves around getting direct feedback from the team for improving the process from Current State and incorporating those changes into the Current State map. Be careful, as this is a destructive process that will change and transform the Current State map into Future State, so you want to make sure you have pictures of the vetted Current State with any changes that the team had requested.

For developing Future State, you will need feedback from the team that identifies issues around the Current State. Give each team member a pad of 3M Post-It Notes® (a.k.a. yellow stickies) and ask them to write one current problem or issue on each sticky. The team should be directed to word their issues in the form of a problem statement, rather than a simple observation. 'Departments don't complete invoices the same way' is much more useful than saying 'Invoices don't match'. Inform the team that this exercise will take fifteen minutes and they should write down as many problems or issues they are aware of. Whenever I conduct these sessions, I always look for around five or more stickies from each team member.

If anyone has used the word "and" on any of their stickies, then that indicates there is more than one problem and two stickies should be used to reflect that. There is no hard and fast rule for how long this takes, but I have found that anything longer than fifteen minutes results in the team losing focus on the task at hand.

At the fifteen-minute mark you want to tell the team to come up to the map and place the stickies on the map where the problem or issue happens. Normally ten minutes is ample time for this exercise.

The next step is for the Mapper to read out each problem or issue from the sticky to the team. The intent here is to make sure the whole team hears the issue and agrees with the point raised. Once the team has agreed, place the sticky back on the map in the same location and move onto the next sticky. As you walk through the process, there will be duplicates of the same problem or issue. Read all the duplicates to the team so that there is agreement around whether they are truly duplicates or, if one or more, are separate issues. Where you have duplicates, the perception of the problem will vary from person to person, so this is a great opportunity to properly frame the issue. In a lot of instances, you will actually rewrite the issue on a separate sticky, guided by the team. You can discard the duplicates that the rewritten sticky replaces (although I prefer to keep them on a separate flipchart until this step is complete). It's always a good idea to mark each sticky as to which one of the Process Boxes it falls under. This will be useful at a later point when we create a Priority Matrix for which problem solutions to execute first.

Now you want to incorporate the changes into the Current State map. You will want the full attention of the group as you want them to come together to discuss the changes to the process. Once the discussion has arrived at a potential solution or change to the process, make the appropriate changes on the map with a marker and move on to the next sticky until all have been covered. Each sticky with an issue will address different parts of the process. As an example, if someone has written a sticky that says 'Sales does not communicate customer billing cycles to Finance', then you would add a process step (guided by feedback from the team) into the Sales & Marketing Process Box along the lines of 'Regional Sales Manager sends customer billing cycle to Finance when contract is signed'. Another example would be removing a redundant process step that would then change Lead time, so you would go ahead and strikeout the Lead time on the Current State map and replace it with the Lead time estimate the group recommends.

Chapter 5: Identifying Opportunities

Having made all the changes to the Current State map, the next step is to remove all the stickies and place them on a blank flipchart or whiteboard. The order in which the stickies are placed on the flipchart is unimportant as you will now direct the team to come up to the flipchart and begin grouping the stickies in common themes. This process is called "Affinitizing". I always direct the group to do this in silence and if there are areas of ambiguity, they can be discussed after grouping the stickies. It may well be that once the stickies are grouped, some of the language used could be ambiguous or too high-level. You will want to rewrite these, or "Scrub" the wording with input from the team.

The purpose of this exercise is to see if there are common, high-level themes that begin to emerge from the multiple problems/issues. As an example, you could have several stickies that point to breakdowns in how the invoice moves from one Process Box to the next. If we look closer at these issues, team discussion could point us to problems with the computerized Accounting System, so our common theme here would be "Accounting System". We can now write "Accounting System" on our flipchart / whiteboard as a heading and put all those stickies under that heading. Continue with creating themes until all the stickies fall under a heading.

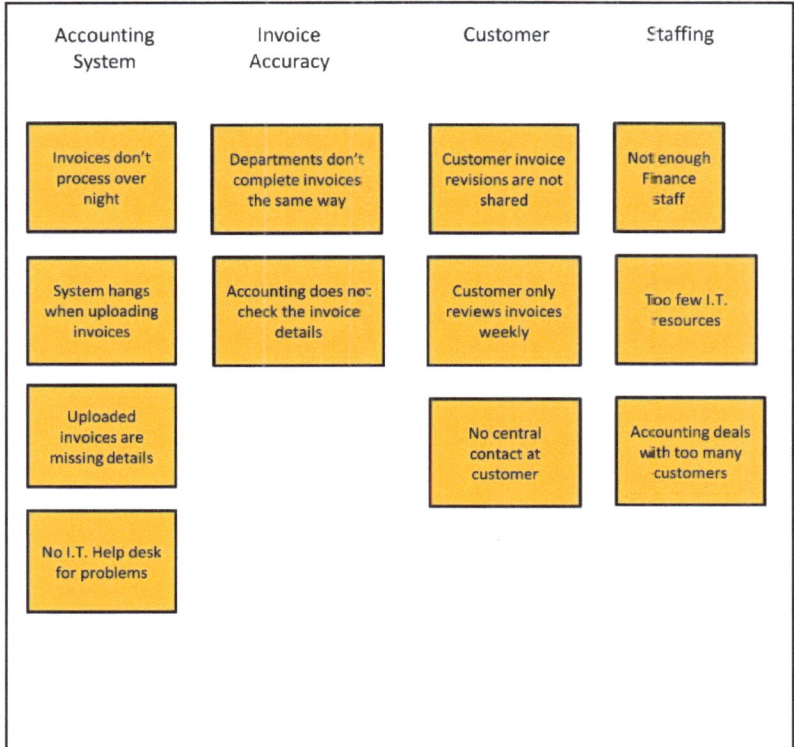

Once the common themes have been identified, the Future State map can be reviewed one last time to make sure that those themes are being addressed on the map.

At this point we can pause and take a look at some of the other data we captured on the map. In the metrics at the bottom of the Process Boxes we listed KPIs, FPY and Process Time. KPIs are a direct measurement of how the process performs and we will use and refer to them throughout the mapping, especially as we begin to identify projects and measure successful execution.

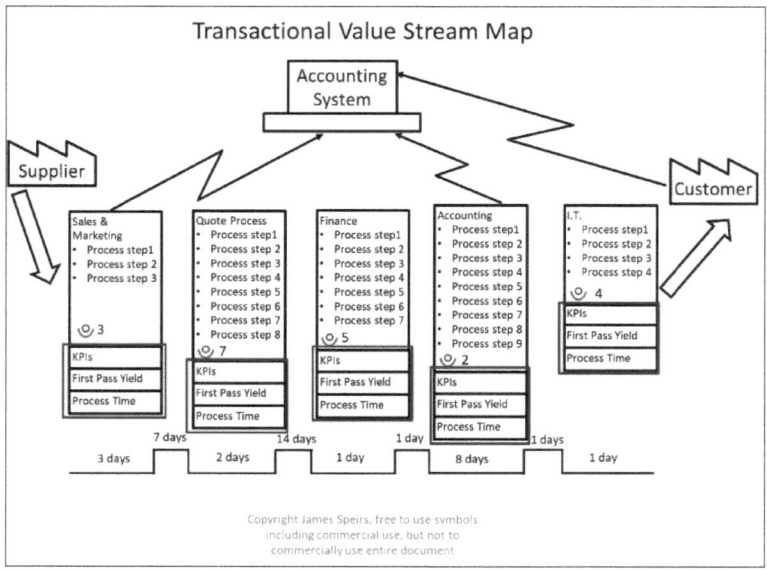

Now we will focus on FPY and calculate Rolled Throughput Yield (RTY), which is an excellent way of seeing how well the overall end-to-end process performs. Normally, it's used in manufacturing, but it can be a profound reality check for the team.

Imagine a VSM with only two Process Boxes. The first process could be Mail Received in the Mail Room and the second process is Mail Delivered to the Post Office. Assume that the Mail Room can only process 80%, or four out of five pieces of mail they receive because there is an incomplete address on the envelope. For the mail delivered to the Post Office, again, only 80% of the mail can go to the Post Office because the Post Office picks up before all the mail is processed. At first glance, it looks as though 80% of everything gets to the end of the process, but it's really only 64%, or less than two out of three.

So how did we get that number? If the Mail Room receives 100 pieces of mail daily and only 80% pass through the first time, then that's 80 pieces of mail that go to the next step. Of those 80 pieces of mail that go to the next step, only 80% of them are picked up by the Post Office, or 64 pieces of mail. In our example, we assume that an invoice with a missing address has to go back to the person that sent the mail to the mail room, rather than the Mail Room being able to rework the invoice themselves. The calculation differs slightly from that used in a manufacturing environment, which experiences scrap, but in the transactional environment, scrap is less of an issue, as the invoice would be reworked.

If we apply that logic to our invoice example and assume each of the five major processes has an 80% FPY, then the RTY is 80% x 80% x 80% x 80% x 80%, which equals 32.7% of invoices that make it through the process to the customer the first time. When most teams see the numbers for their RTY, it is always an eye-opener for how their process performs. RTY helps the team focus on areas where breakdowns occur and may affect how they decide project prioritization. In the above example, I used 80% FPY for each Process Box for ease of calculation. When you do your map, you will find that FPY will vary across each of the processes.

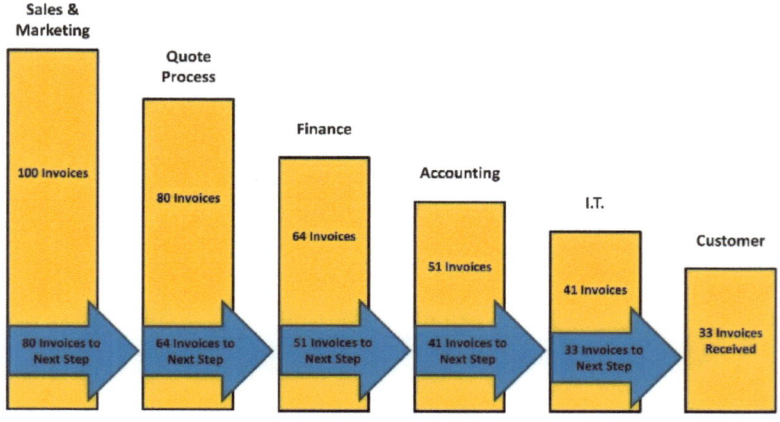

Moving to the next metric, Process Time, we can calculate what the total Value Add is for each Process Box and the overall end-to-end Value Stream. In the Lean Six Sigma world, if a process doesn't add value to what you produce or the customer wouldn't pay for it, then why do it? Earlier we got the Process Time and Lead Time from our SMEs for each Process Box. To calculate the percent Value Added, simply divide Process Time by Lead Time and multiply by 100. Look at the Sales & Marketing Process Box in our example (page 34). We know the Lead Time is three days. Let's assume the Process Time involved is one day and with simple mathematics we can see that 1 day divided by 3 days multiplied by 100 is 33%. In executing this process, we only added 33% value, telling us that 67% of the time (100% minus 33%) we don't add value to the output of the process.

Value Add for the entire Value Stream is calculated by adding *all* the Process Times together and dividing by *all* the Lead Times *plus all* the Queue Times. This will give you the Value-Added time for the end-to-end Value Stream.

The team can now use the throughput and value-add measurements to more finely tune how they view the problems or issues and this will help with their prioritizations.

With all the problems or issues agreed upon and the language "scrubbed", the problems or issues can then be prioritized by the order in which they should be executed. Each problem or issue can be either entered into a spreadsheet in real-time or simply written on a flipchart or whiteboard. If you have access to a projector, using a spreadsheet is an easy way to let the team see how the prioritization progresses, otherwise, use a whiteboard or flipchart.

The prioritization method I use here is based on the concept of a "Risk Priority Number" and is a technique taken from Failure Mode Effect Analysis (FMEA). For this exercise you want three major headings that will affect how each of the problems or issues will be executed. Three examples could be Project Cost, Project Effort and Customer Satisfaction. Effort and Cost are standards you want to incorporate as these will tell you the level of Effort required to complete the project and Cost will tell you how much the project will cost. For each of these you want to assign a number from 1 to 3.

For Cost, if the project will incur a high cost, you want to score a 1, for low cost, assign a 3. Anything in the middle would be scored a 2. Repeat this for Effort with 1 being high effort, 2 is medium and 3 is low effort. For Customer Satisfaction the opposite applies, low Customer Satisfaction scores a 1, average impact is scored 2 and a high impact to Customer Satisfaction scores a 3. When you run through this exercise, it's important to point out to the team that the priorities assigned to each of the three headings are "best guesstimates". Obviously, you can't stop for two hours while someone figures out how much a project will cost, or calls the customer to see how important the project would be in improving their satisfaction with the process.

To arrive at the RPN, the three numbers are multiplied together. The projects are then ranked from high to low score and the highest scoring projects are the ones to focus on first. For example, high Cost would be a 1, high Effort would score a 1 and low Customer Satisfaction would score a 1; 1x1x1=1. At the other end of the scale, low Cost would be 3, low Effort scores a 3 and high Customer Satisfaction scores 3 also; 3x3x3=27.

In the real world, this ranking may not be completely realistic, as you may find that there are lower scoring projects that must be completed first in order to allow the execution of other high scoring projects. These are referred to as "Enabling" projects, as they *enable* you to complete the others when you have finished these lower scoring projects. A good example would be changes to an I.T. system. Effort and Cost here could both score low (high Effort and high Cost) and result in no obvious improvement in Customer Satisfaction (1x1x1=1), but in order to have a correct invoice sent to the customer, this project would need to be completed first.

The final part of the project review is to assign Project Owners to each of the projects. The Project Owner will be the person that takes on the project and sees it through to completion. They will be responsible for assigning resources where needed, setting the project timeline and scheduling meetings. Normally project meetings will take place on a weekly basis, but dependent on the scope and complexity of the project, meetings could occur every two weeks. Most importantly, the Project Owners will want to keep the momentum going. Without regular meetings it's easy to lose focus and then the project will begin to falter or stall.

At this point you should have a complete list of all the projects, prioritized by RPN and the approval of the group to move forward with all the projects. It's not necessary to start all the projects at once and more than likely resource limitations would not allow all the projects to start simultaneously. For the projects that are not starting, there should be an agreed upon start date and this should be captured in the Project List.

Execution Order	Value Stream	Problem Statement	Start Date	Finish Date	Project Owner	Project Benefit	Prioritization			Overall Priority
							Cost 1 - Low 3 - High	Customer Satisfaction 1 - Low 3 - High	Effort 1 - High 3 - Low	
1	Finance	Invoice approval takes 3 days	5/15/2017	8/15/2017	Ken Murphy	Remove 2 days from processing	3	3	3	27
2	Sales & Marketing	Sales do not communicate customer billing cycle	5/15/2017	7/1/2017	Mary Smith	Eliminate rework by Finance	1	3	2	6
3	I.T.	Electronic invoices are batched taking an extra 24 hours to reach the customer	5/15/2017	9/1/2017	Mike O'Brien	Improve Customer Satisfaction	2	3	1	6

Again, reaching consensus across projects is important, as you want the group to agree on the direction, moving forward. It's not necessary to have complete agreement across the board, but you need the majority of the group to approve that direction.

Once the final version of the map has been created have the entire team sign the completed Future State Map. It can be displayed prominently in the department so others can see the Future State. The team now has ownership of what they have created and should be proud of their work!

Chapter 6: Executing Initiatives

From all the work that you have put into the mapping process, it may seem that the difficult part has been completed, but the truth is that you are now moving into what is the defining part of the mapping process. Many times, the energy is lost at this point, since it seems all the heavy lifting has been done. Given the effort the group has put into the mapping, they may tend to see the process as being complete. However, putting structure around the projects and their execution allows you to ensure the continued success of the improvement process and underlines the importance of completing the identified projects. At this point Future State has not been realized and will only become a reality when the projects that get you to that point are complete.

The prioritized list of projects now takes over from the Project Charter as your main document and will let you create a realistic timeline for execution. Since each of the projects have been identified as falling under specific project boxes from the VSM and Project Owners have been assigned, you now have a list of the individuals that will facilitate the changes. Your role now changes from the Value Stream Mapper to that of Project Manager and it falls to you to create the structure around the project execution. Generally, you will want to focus on the top four or five projects, or at a minimum, the projects that affect the bulk of the change. Arrange one-on-one meetings with the group members that have been assigned projects and work with them to develop a realistic timeline for when the project will be completed, any additional resources they may need and what the significant milestones are. It's important to realize that the projects from the Mapping have been assigned to team members who may have little or no experience leading a project, so your role will be that of supporting their efforts to ensure success.

Moving forward, you will want to schedule weekly Tollgate (or Project Review) meetings to review the progress for all the current projects. For these meetings you will want to include the group members that have been assigned projects and the Value Stream Champion. In the Execute phase, the role of the Value Stream Champion is still the same; they are the person that removes obstacles and ensures continued progress of the projects.

The Project Prioritization list can now be expanded to include the date the project started, the anticipated completion date and a project status indicator. The status indicator can be simple text, "On-track", "Off-track" or "Stalled" and can be colored green, yellow and red, for visual impact (see the example on the next page) The project is deemed "Off-track" if the current progress is not being met, but the problem is being corrected or corrective actions are being put in place. If the project is "Stalled", this means that progress has halted and the only way to get the project back on track is with the intervention of the Champion or the Project Manager. It's important to recognize the differences of the two statuses, as there can often be a fine line between them. Discussing the issue with the Champion may be necessary to clearly define where things stand.

Execution Order	Value Stream	Problem Statement	Start Date	Finish Date	Project Owner	Project Benefit	Project Status	Project Update	Prioritization			Overall Priority
									Cost 1 - Low 3 - High	Customer Satisfaction 1 - Low 3 - High	Effort 1 - High 3 - Low	
1	Finance	Invoice approval takes 3 days	5/15/2017	8/15/2017	Ken Murphy	Remove 2 days from processing	On-Track	Project waiting for management approval to implement	3	3	3	27
2	Sales & Marketing	Sales do not communicate customer billing cycle	5/15/2017	7/1/2017	Mary Smith	Eliminate rework by Finance	Stalled	Project halted due to Annual Sales Conference	1	3	2	6
3	I.T.	Electronic invoices are batched taking an extra 24 hours to reach the customer	5/15/2017	9/1/2017	Mike O'Brien	Improve Customer Satisfaction	Off-Track	Project needs additional resources	2	3	1	6

The meetings continue until all the projects have reached the desired outcome.

Chapter 7: Implementing Controls

As each of the projects are completed, there should be controls put in place to make sure that none of the progress is lost. Typically, the control mechanisms are in the form of metrics or KPIs that are reviewed on an on-going basis, whether it is weekly or monthly, depending on the ability to access the data and the process change that was put into place. For more granular processes, weekly would be advisable. As the processes being measured increase in complexity, it becomes less easy to get reliable data in a timely fashion. If the KPI or metric is around daily processing, then weekly reporting would be sufficient. For measuring a process that can only access weekly data, then reporting on a monthly basis would fulfill the requirement. There are no hard and fast rules for KPIs for the Control phase, but you want to make sure that the improvements that were made are still benefitting the process. A typical Control Plan is shown below:

Value Stream	Project Benefit	Project Owner	KPI	October	November	December	January
Finance	Remove 2 days from processing	Ken Murphy	Finance Lead Time less than 1 Day	On-Track	On-Track	On-Track	On-Track
Sales & Marketing	Eliminate rework by Finance	Mary Smith	Less than 15% Invoice Rework	On-Track	On-Track	Off-Track	On-Track
I.T.	Improve Customer Satisfaction	Mike O'Brien	No Customer Invoice complaints	On-Track	On-Track	On-Track	On-Track

For this example, the metrics were captured on a monthly basis for three examples of on-going projects. Control Plans can be easily set up in MS Excel and color coding can be used to show if the control metric is either on or off track. For ease of illustration, the example above shows tracking the control for four months, but you would want to track the Control Plan for a full twelve months.

It is not necessary to have monthly meetings with the team to review the Control phase status, but at the very least you would want to give a monthly update to the Champion. Should any of the implemented projects show that they are "Off-track", then you would want to meet with the Project

Owner to determine the severity of the issue and then either continue to monitor or escalate to the Champion, if it needs to be.

Summary

At this point we have followed the improvement journey from the initial mapping, through identifying and executing projects to making sure that the improvements continue to reap benefits. Nothing we have covered is rocket science. Nothing that can't be created with blank paper and a marker (or pen).

Probably the most important factor for success is being able to approach the Value Stream, not allow yourself to be intimidated by it and be confident of a positive and successful outcome. What I have gone over in this book is a relatively high-level approach that will get you up and running with a Transactional Value Stream Map. I intentionally did not cover all the multiple symbols that can be used, but rather wanted the reader to be able to execute a map without being caught up in a lot of the details that typically are not used in the Transactional world.

Since all processes continually evolve (or devolve), the Value Stream should be reassessed at least twice a year. This could be as simple an exercise as reviewing with the Champion or, if it has been determined that there have been changes in personnel, systems and other areas, then this could trigger another Mapping Event. The event would start with the Future State map from the first Mapping Event. Projects previously executed to get to Future State means that your previous Future State is now your Current State and building a Preliminary Map would not be necessary.

If the business wants to dig further into individual processes, then it's entirely possible to take one of the Process Boxes from the VSM and create another individual VSM around that Process Box. After all, this is Continuous Improvement!

Everything I have covered in this book are proven methods that have worked effectively for me in the past. Remember, I would not have developed this approach if I had not been challenged to adapt and streamline the mapping process. If you adopt the same frame of mind, you too will be successful.

Good luck!

Glossary

- 3M Post-It Notes® - Self-adhesive notes, affectionately known as "Stickies"
- Affinitizing – Grouping information together into common themes
- Back-Office Processes – Processes within the business that support other areas of the business
- Butcher Paper – Originally sold to Butchers for wrapping meat, it is used in a variety of ways in education and is also known as "Craft Paper"
- Control Plan – Underlying plan to make sure that process changes are being maintained
- Current State Map – Value Stream Map of how the current process functions
- Executing Initiatives - The act of working on individual improvement projects
- External Customer – The "End" Customer, outside of the business
- Failure Mode Effect Analysis (FMEA) – Technique used in design, manufacturing or assembly process to determine potential process breakdowns and the severity of their impact
- First Pass Yield – Percentage of the time the process works, as intended, the first time

- Future State Map – Value Stream Map of how the process will look in the future, based on improvements to the Current State
- Gemba Walk – Observing how the process works, where the work takes place, first hand
- Ice-Breaker exercise – A brief five to ten-minute activity at the beginning of a meeting to warm up the group
- Ideal State Map – Utopian view of how the process would look in a perfect world
- Identifying Opportunities – Process of finding potential projects that will benefit the process
- Implementing Controls – Putting measures in place to ensure changes to the process take effect
- Information Flows – Part of the Value Stream Map that shows how information moves across the Value Stream
- Internal Customer – The Customer inside the business
- Lead Time – Amount of time taken for a process from start to finish, including all delays and rework
- Lean Six Sigma Black Belt – Improvement Expert trained in all the necessary tools
- Lean Six Sigma Green Belt - Improvement Expert trained in most, but not all the necessary tools
- Lean Six Sigma Master Black Belt - Improvement Expert trained in all the necessary tools and trains Green and Black Belts
- Mapper - The person that facilitates the Mapping Event and all associated activities

- Mapping Event – The meeting where the Value Stream Map is vetted and Ideal and Future State maps are created
- Non-Value Added – The amount of time that the process does not add any value for the Customer
- Off-Track – Defined as when a project is not proceeding as planned
- On-Track – When the project is proceeding as planned
- Parking Lot – Tool for capturing additional ideas on a flipchart or white board
- Planning and Prework – The initial work that lays the foundation for the Mapping Event
- Preliminary Mapping – Creating the Current State Value Stream Map from Subject Matter Expert feedback
- Priority Matrix – A tool for organizing project execution, most impactful first
- Problem Statement – A sentence that describes what the problem is, where it occurs, who it affects and when
- Process and Metric Boxes – Graphic boxes on the Value Stream Map that list high level process steps in the order they occur and quantifiable measurements of that process
- Process Map – Detailed map of individual process steps at a granular level
- Project Charter – Guiding document that lists, at a minimum, the Champion, Problem Statement, Project Scope, Team Members and their managers

- Project Scope – Defines the start and end of the process
- Queue Time – Amount of time that elapses between Process Boxes
- Risk Priority Number – Overall project ranking based on three criteria; Effort, Cost and Customer Satisfaction (although the three can be modified to meet the project needs)
- Rolled Throughput Yield – Multiplication of First Pass Yields to give an overall picture of the time the process executes through the Value Stream
- Stalled – Project has halted
- Subject Matter Expert (SME) – The person closest to the process that actually does the work
- Supplier and Customer Boxes – Graphic boxes on the left and right of the Value Stream Map that show the Supplier to the process and the End-Customer of the process
- Tollgate Meeting – Regularly scheduled Project Review meeting to review the progress of project execution
- Transactional process – Processes, that are not tangible, that take place in the business
- Trusted Advisor – Person that has the skills and the business knowledge to assist the Champion
- Value Added - The amount of time that the process adds value for the Customer, also defined as 'would the Customer pay for this?'

- Value Stream Champion – Executive Sponsor of the Value Stream Map and associated events
- Value Stream Map – End to end view of the process, displayed as a map

Step by Step Guide

Planning and Prework

- Determine Value Stream Champion
- Determine Problem Statement
- Determine Project Scope
- Determine Team members (SMEs) and Managers
- Complete the Project Charter

Preliminary Mapping

- Interview the first SME
- Draw the first Process Box, Metrics and Times on the Preliminary Map
- Interview next SME
- Draw the next Process Box, Metrics and Times on the Preliminary Map
- Repeat interview process until Preliminary Map is complete
- Review Preliminary Map with each SME
- Print (or Draw) Current State map full size
- Conduct Gemba Walk with each SME
- Send out Agenda
- Schedule Mapping Event

Mapping Event

- Review Current State Map
- Create Ideal State Map
- Create Future State Map
- Identify Opportunities
- Prioritize Opportunities
- Assign Opportunities

Executing Initiatives

- Execute Initiatives
- Schedule Tollgate Meetings
- Hold Tollgate Meetings
- Complete Initiatives

Implementing Controls

- Create Control Plan
- Review Control Plan with Champion

www.ingramcontent.com/pod-product-compliance
Lightning Source LLC
Chambersburg PA
CBHW040321220526
45473CB00009B/2526